and then we became

and then we became

devorah major

City Lights Books | San Francisco

Cover design by em dash

"nommo—how we came to speak" previously published in *Bum Rush the Page: a def poetry jam,* 2001

"cosmology meditation #1" and "history of the canary island whistlers" previously published in *Penbroke Magazine* #39, 2007

"yes to life" previously published in *Incantations and Rites,* Artichoke Press, 2013

"brown lady in white" previously published in *Brown Glass Windows,* Curbstone Press, 2002

"ben lomond" previously published in *100 Parades,* CPITS, 2000

"tempest" previously published in *Ocean Voices: An Anthology of Ocean Poems,* Spinner Publications, 2013

"janice dolores" previously published in *Cave Canem Anthology #3,* 1998

"war memories" previously published in *Sometimes in the Open,* Sacramento Poetry Center Press, 2009

"on issues of aliens, immigration and cosmology" previously published in *Poetry of Resistance: Voices for Social Justice,* University of Arizona Press, 2016

Library of Congress Cataloging-in-Publication Data
Names: Major, Devorah, 1952- author.
Title: And then we became / Devorah Major.
Description: San Francisco : City Lights Books, [2016] | Includes
  bibliographical references and index.
Identifiers: LCCN 2016022748 | ISBN 9780872867260 (paperback)
Subjects: | BISAC: POETRY / American / African American. | POETRY /
  American
  / General.
Classification: LCC PS3563.A3915 A6 2016 | DDC 811/.54—dc23
LC record available at https://lccn.loc.gov/2016022748

City Lights books are published at the City Lights Bookstore
261 Columbus Avenue, San Francisco, CA 94133
www.citylights.com

Contents

spirit

other selves

fragile

whole

and then we became

spirit

cosmology meditation #1

we are the memory
of that place without measure
that filled all space
that never was and ever will be

that place existing as the perfect note
yet making no sound
holding all colors inside a light
that was nothing but darkness

we are the memory of a breath
that could not be but was
a breath that swelled to bubble
that burst and then collapsed

we are the memory
gestated in days that lasted eons
as the universe womb birthed heat light
rock ice mineral song us

we are the impossible made flesh
creating infinite possibilities of hope
or endless chasms of despair
inside the prayers which we have become

nommo
how we come to speak

before a generation
passed we
children of the third word
knew how to take
the gift of language
contort it crimson
and sew it to our teeth

how we mangle
this tongue that needs
unending translation

we require it to be
a constantly changing chameleon
a hypnotist, a con man, a cheat

with words we manufacture demons
who devour souls and erase memory
look at how often we honor speech

that can make us hate
that can cause us to deny
our mothers
our brothers
our self

we have articulated
a deadly weapon
that subverts knowledge
and betrays faith

so how now
do we

again learn to listen
with more than ears

at once try to speak
with more than tongue

how now
do we

put our tongues back
in our mouths

Nommo: *Deity from the Malian Dogon cosmology who was created by their Supreme deity, Amma, and possesses the power to create by the spoken word. As an African philosophical concept, nommo refers to the generative or procreative power of the spoken word.*

year of the dragon

last year was the year of not dying

the bougainvillea startled me
with its few wilting leaves hidden
beneath a spray of thorns and tendrils

the lemon tree stripped of its hard fruit
branches bent and torn wept its leaves yellow
onto the sandy dirt below not sure
if it would blossom this spring

my father's heart vibrated
buzzed hummed fluttered
but could not maintain
measured beats

we held our breath
as winter touched us softly
met january in stillness
tired and battered
counting heads
to find we were all here
once again

maybe next year will be
the year of forgiving
or the year of rejoining
or the year of silence

it's an abstract constellation we live in
knowing the clock will turn
at any moment
and it will suddenly become
the year of passing on
the year of roads that end

but this year
this year is the year
we survived
the year of not dying

the yes to life

i did
ask to be born

when i was in that universal space
between where i had been and here
when i was riding on x star in y galaxy
on the plateau where birth
meets passing on
i know
i was one who pulsed
shone sang cajoled yelled
cried and pled yes
yes i want a tongue
yes i want to breathe
yes i want to dance

i want to be born

of course, i didn't know
what i was asking for
had no idea of hunger or pain
could not conceive of the word for despair
or the thought of utter aloneness

had yet to understand
how suffer and celebration
could sleep so close together

no i didn't know
but i begged and begged
until i got what i asked for
every tongue tip mouth full
feather touch soft belly
pitted crag, breezy, gravelly
moment out of life

i wanted it then
i want it now

human

under the brightest full moon

i am less than a microscopic speck
on the edge of the universe's lens

how can a grain of sand be sentient
how can a drop of rain dream

but here i am, singing through the night

and then we became
other selves

the judge

the judge moaned that it was
women who made him bitter
and later wept that just

this day his daughter had
pulled a knife on him
when he tried to talk to her

without reason   he said

was ready to cut

he knit a silence
where his questions
should have lived

i counseled him to try
honey and sweat
without too much salt

brown lady in white

have you seen her?
she is shadows of africa buried
under a mausoleum of whiteness
her gingerbread skin cracks through
the white paint she brushes
over her cheeks
across her forehead
down her neck

to meet a blouse of white
a long white skirt
white stockings
white sneakers
a white cape blanketing
away cold and rain mists

she walks engulfed by white
cutting the air so quickly
that when she passes
she is often unseen

i have seen her
scurrying down mission street
gusting through the tenderloin
pushing past crowds on market

a friend swears she has seen
her in harlem and another
claims to have caught a glimpse
of her in downtown atlanta

have you seen her
is she one of many?

she cannot become the whiteness
she wraps around herself

her skin tones break through
proclaiming color
brown, they insist
when we were young, they sing
as they rise above the paint
when we were younger
we glowed in many browns

she argues with her shadow
cuts the air with aspersions
her steps are short and clipped
as she flies down the street
a whirl of discord
brown still
under the white

have you seen her
walking faster and faster still
until she almost disappears
shining brown
under the layers
of white

amina's trial

1. unrebuked testimony

when she was fourteen
i gave my daughter over to a man

who offered fine cloth and chickens, a goat
and a proposal of marriage.

it is not because i did not love her
but because she was too beautiful

because she held her head so high
danced so freely, as if we were not poor

because she had started to bleed
and her eyes were dangerous

dark and brooding like his
when they traveled over her small hard breasts.

when she became woman and mother and mate
she declared her body as her own, so of course he left her.

she has been faithful as daughter, as mother, as sister
but as wife, her spirit has betrayed her,
as i always knew it would.

2. unneeded testimony

i divorce thee. i divorce thee. i divorce thee, i said years ago
when i moved from her door without reaching back.

i did not care then. i do not care now,
because her eyes had turned bitter, her mouth become salt

because her dowry was spent, her demands unending
she is no longer my wife. i have no part in this.

3. unspoken testimony

yes, i have tried to be the name,
the name my mother gave me.

ask anyone and they will tell you
an honest woman, amina

trustworthy amina, sure,
dependable, believable amina.

yes i know the father of this child
remember his gaze

like hot breath
on my feet, my hands, my neck.

because i needed a husband
since the first had abandoned me

i did not lift my eyes until he promised
but when he made the oath of future marriage

sealed it in the name of allah
i unwrapped my hair.

4. damning testimony

yes i was her boyfriend, but not the father.
she was not married then; she is not married now.

of the child she has borne i can say nothing,
because i am not the father and will not share her fate.

i will help you to dig her hole, if you want
right there on the path where we first crossed.

when i asked her to raise her eyes to mine
she turned away, but i saw an edge of smile.

i will dig it there until it is over four feet deep
so only her head will rise above the dirt

and those brown river eyes in which i swam,
in which i almost drowned, will stare straight out.

the hole will not be too wide, as her shoulders are slim
and the breasts that now feed her child will be flat and dry

if need be i will pick up the first stone heavy and sharp
and i will hurl it smooth and sure at that woman

all the while proclaiming the greatness of god
all the while declaring that i am not the father.

lady bombardier's desire

i can bomb as well as any man
the female air force lieutenant
tells the reporter
barbed wire in the edges of her voice
so all will hear that she can bomb

        barrage
        crush
        decimate
        demolish
        annihilate

iraqi babies
sudanese mothers
slavic elders
chinese workers

        any target
        named as enemy

she is woman

        yes

but she is soldier first
and women's liberation
is not her issue

her point is aptitude

she aced basic training
flies with the best
knows that she can

                                bomb as well as
                                if not better than
                                any man

all she wants
is the chance

any name will do

"Of the mother of Our Lady nothing is certainly known."
Butler's *Lives of the Saints*

when my mother spoke of ann's kitchen
(or perhaps it was hannah
no one seems completely sure)
she baked memories of cinnamon
and crowns of powdered sugar
her grandmother became saint ann
like the name on the door
of the room where i stayed

a room valued for wide windows
where i could spend early mornings
lolling in the firm fingers of the sun

i almost never think of the one known
only by my mother's folded memories
woven like fine white lace
patterned and full of holes

she came to america as a teenager
left hillsides and country paths
spoke to her husband in a tongue
that was not her own

turned the dinner plate face down
to eat some butter on her corn
made new traditions
in her transplanted home

her husband fought to see us once
filled my face with silvery wet
moustache kisses squeezed me
so tight i could not breathe
except through his love

an offering of ann's cookies
brimming with butter, candied cherries
finely sifted flour, sparkling sugar
was layered in two tins
passed from him to my mother to us

but anna, or was it hannah
never could admit us
into her world, shwartza
her neighbors would see us
dark, like the richest of earth
or the night sky that held her dreams
or the dirt you wash from your feet
before you climb into a tight-sheeted bed

we were not to come into her world
and she would not enter ours

she is mine, as i am hers
but we never knew each other
my name is black
hers fear and regret

history of the canary island whistlers

needing to show what would happen
to enslaved ones who used language
as weapon, as poultice, as plow

but afraid to kill those
whose mouths held spells and danger

spanish soldiers cut out their tongues
and put those men adrift in a worn boat
confident that the atlantic
would open her gaping mouth
and swallow those ominous souls

but decades after the leaky boat landed
on canary island shores
if you walked across a mountain ridge
of that rocky tree-filled island

you could hear those tongue-less men
whistling their sadness and joy in spanish
shaping the air into foreign consonants and vowels
modulating alien tones into verbs and nouns
becoming a new species of black birds
who would not be silenced
and could not be killed

city scat

we come to this city
of concrete, brick
steel and toil

country people
knowing the earth

sea-faring people
reading the tides

gambling people
holding jokers and spades

we come to this city

hard laughin'
weep sob wailin'
prayin' celebratin' people
bending and sweating

we come to
this hiss crack
slap snap
siren whirl
holler
electric zip

and burn
city

rounding
bustling corners
banging our heads
against destiny
and crumbling
brick walls of confusion

we come to this city
that can cage us
enrage us
deny us
revile us
turn us
from friends and family
into prey and predator

we live in this city
this hip howl
she bop
da he bop
da we bop
bang clang
swinging city

we come to this city
and we name it ours

and then we became
fragile

losing limbs

1.
such simple things
these hands

that are cup and sieve
scissor and cloth
mallet and fan

open lotus blossoms
and dark-lined clam shells

they have torn and beat
cleaned and caressed
shuddered and bled

charted with love
the map of my hands
is my journey

2.
such simple things
these feet

the scars of my ancestors
cut into their soles
carrying more
than bones, blood and sinew

as they climbed and wept
danced and stumbled
held kisses and rubbed comfort
bristled and stung

drum and hammer
ladder and cushion

these feet have loved
sand and water
oil and touch

3.
lucky to have lived he lies still
nothing but memory beneath his trunk

4.
she hides the missing leg
beneath bulbous skirts

5.
there was no granddaughter's
tiny foot or curled finger to kiss
before they laid her under

6.
such simple things
these hands
these feet
these limbs
these lives
these broken leaves

mother to mother
for Brendalisa

pick up the phone

your daughter
wants you to
wrap love around her name
when you hear her voice

she cries prayers into the receiver
pleads for you to hear
how he touched her
how he tore her
how he bruised her

and she knows
he is your husband

your daughter chants heartache
into the disconnected line
begging that you understand
how he betrayed her
how he blamed her
how he broke her

and she knows
he is her father

your daughter wants you to know
she does not blame you

she knows how one can
love a damaged soul

she loves him
she loves you
she is trying to learn
to love herself

war memories
for Jessica

i have forgotten myself.
who i was
i can not now know
who i have become
is a stranger.

there are other things
to lose in battle
besides arms and legs
eyes and gut
other sacrifices
before life.

i have lost myself.

i am not who i was
before this war.
i am not she
who dares to be.

my mother is so happy
with this worn body
returned home.

we pretend
that i am as whole as i look.

but at night
when i stare through the dark
at the hidden image in the mirror
i cannot lie to the stranger i see.

i have forgotten everything
except my affection for children
my service to country
and my insatiable fear.

for makmoud of gaza

the world slowed with heat from the blaze of the sun
as he loped toward the bird in the haze of the sun

though their caged music often made him cry in the sun
he strove to catch songbirds flying toward the sun

he felt a fluttering heart between palms warmed by the sun
listened with teardrops to the bird's plaintive song of the sun

his thirteen-year-old chest exploded in the setting of his sun
a vision of feathers, wet and blackened-red, etched in the sun

can we know the soldier's heart dried by the weight of the sun
who killed a boy chasing songbirds in the sway of the sun

haiti photographer

my brother was struck by lightning, lifted up
carried from camera and rock to tree, closer to the falls.
sacred waters thundered down the mountainside
as the people sang praise and promise to damballah.

carried from camera and rock to tree, closer to the falls
he looked with different eyes, forever changed.
as the people sang praise and promise to damballah
he was given fire blessings or a curse that would devour.

he looked with different eyes, forever changed
his lens of experience shattered and reshaped
filled with fire blessings or a curse that would devour
seared with the truth of miracles' inevitable scars.

with his lens of experience shattered and reshaped
magic unused mushroomed inside his soul,
seared with the truth of miracles' inevitable scars
leaving tremors and trembles, stumbling footsteps

magic unused mushroomed inside his soul
while sacred waters thundered down the mountainside
leaving tremors and trembles, stumbling footsteps
my brother was struck by lightning, lifted up

sketching dementia

a cushion of forgetting
a warble of gauze fingers

a warble of gauze fingers
a stumble of paint brushes

a stumble of paintbrushes
a startle of bitter scotch

a cushion of forgetting

a startle of bitter scotch
days flavored with no rhythm

days flavored with no rhythm
open newspaper half-read

open newspaper half-read
the past a paper snowflake

a startle of bitter scotch

the past a paper snowflake
another friend now buried

another friend now buried
another face is blurred

another face is blurred
every day tremble full

the past a paper snowflake

newtown interview

it's over now, the reporter tells
the seven year old, red-rim-eyed girl
you know that, he asks, tells, asks, tells
her. she looks at him with her good girl face
with her please the teacher tip of head
as he repeats himself again,
it's over now, you know that
right? he is trying to make her believe.
but she had already forsaken the easter bunny,
has serious doubts about santa claus,
and two front teeth gone, money found
under her pillow, she suspects that
the tooth fairy looks just like her mom

her eyes grow bigger
she finds the smallest smile
forces it to grow
yet she knows
in a corner of her belly
that has never hurt like this before
that it is not over

but if the stranger with the
microphone and camera
wants to believe it is over
she does too

when he turns to interview
the next person
she curls into mommy's arms

stroke journey

1.

thick
cold and blinding
white
strangely dry

there is no self
arms, legs, breath, thought
disappear

endless flat expanses
no trees
no rivers or seas
no points from which to navigate

no color but white

whose lips that slur and groan
whose eyes that will not stay open
whose legs that cannot walk
whose mind that cannot remember

where is he

2.

red the fear
red the tears
red the frustration
red the fury
red the resolve

a face comes into view
there is love
red and pulsing

3.

once there were
letters words phrases
codes broken at a glance
now hieroglyphics turned to
ideogram turned to cyrillic
transformed to child scribbles
haunting in their mystery

where does a writer go
when there are no words
that can be read
only symbols written
in an alien tongue

my life he cries
this is my life
inside these words
i cannot read
around these letters
i do not know

my life

4.

he does not reach for the past
it is not there

squamous cell

it is patient and ravenous
in its appetite for my mother

it has nibbled on her cheek
nipped her back
bitten deeply into one calf
gnawed repeatedly
on the backs of her hands

growing hard and firm
inside the spider-veined
fabric of her translucent skin

again and again
she endures being cut
notched and wedged
burnt, gouged and sliced

but like the tide each evening
it comes back, spreads
its tongue across her flesh
and finds new places to sup

janice dolores

at her ending, my cousin said,
blood dripped
from her mother's fingertips
the ones sculpted
and painted vamp red
in contrast to her always
balanced gold-tipped filter cigarette.

the blood spilt out of her gums
and over her cracked lips
which until then were kept
painted thick and round
in bubbling red.

was her future betrayed by a seer
who told her mother the only way
was to hide the girl's true name?
this only child of an only child
who was to birth an only child.

continuing a line of daughters
who kept their love in tightly
sealed amber bottles
each remembering
a different shade of red
that concealed dreams.

when her cards were read
was the empress reversed?
when thrown did the cowries
always fall face down?
did the coconut shells clatter out
sixteen darkened fragments of no?
could she have gone a different way
and worn a gentler shade?

this lady of sorrows
this woman of bridled tears
who bled until there was
no red left to bleed
no red to stop a wound
that wouldn't heal.

ruby tears spent
while yearning
to find the glistening spirit
who once was named dolores.

old soldier

i notice his legs first
splayed like a young colt's
rocky body tottering
barely able to balance

moments later i see his head
thick with uncombed silver kinks
and his dusty walnut brown
hands grabbing onto
an overloaded grocery cart

his age fluctuates as i watch

until it becomes an algorithm
that can only be factored

by multiplying
all of the wars he has fought
by each of the battles he has
though often wounded
survived

emergency room visitation

she is back
closer than ever
sleek and smooth, bleached
white bones showing through
her dark cloak

somehow she has draped her
bony limbs around his body
as he lies on the gurney
coughing while pulling air
into his tired lungs

she knows i can see her
as she whispers into his ear
of how patient she has been
with his constant rebuffs
always pushing her away
these last few years

but now she cannot contain her ardor
nor the chill of her promise

this night she places her head near his
dryly sucks at his tremulous lips
inhales his breath and begins to glow

he begins to talk to me
of stories written but unfinished
essays published but lost
files i must find and read
books i must discover
works he would have me complete

i nod and smile, promise and cajole

we have been in this land
of beeps and groans
efficiency and bandages
false sterility and long tubing
many, many times

she grows fatter
as she strokes his cheeks
kisses the tears on the corners
of his eyes

the nurses and doctors join me
as we each take one of her limbs
and start to pry her loose

their job is to deny death her meal this night
mine to cover the moment with love

she releases her grip one more time
rises from the bed as if suddenly
remembering another appointment
then bends and kisses his mouth full on

i do not want to look, yet am frozen
staring into the glaring smile of death

ben lomond

crickets scratch their legs together
tree frogs call in the moon
and my daughter lies covered in sweat

golden and polished she blends in
with the oiled knotty pine walls.

i cannot see her breath soft
between slender arms
thrown wide across the bed.

mouth cracked and silent
she heals herself.

and then we became
whole

yoruba woman

1.

i don't know if you would
recognize me as yours
if we met in my now
but i am glad to be this me
born in america
carib, irish, slavic, jew born
african woman that i be

this is not to say
that i am glad you were stolen
or celebrate the way you
were torn from your bloodline
stripped of your legacy
betrayed

i do not revel
in the loneliness
that kept your lips tight
your back hard
your heart scarred

but the me that is
that weaves these strands

that finds me free
and headstrong

the loudmouth me
wide hipped frizzy hair
soft belly me
who has found a home
inside this peanut skin
would not be here
without your crossing

2.

they tell me you were mean
sultry dark skin
fine-boned hands
that stirred the pot
hung between the three legs
of the african stove
you made the irish man build
so that you could cook outside
under stars that spread across
the skies in foreign constellations

they say you would stand near
the caribbean beach and
stare at the sea

hold water under your tongue
your back to the ocean
that could have led you home

i'm told you were cruel
silent and strong
an obeah woman
(before it wore that name)
burying ifa beneath
the arching avocado tree

3.

one year
landed in england
i took the train to liverpool
walked crowded streets
to the harbor's mouth
where tales are told
of the ships they built
the cargo they carried

and deep underground i
explored their newly crafted
model of a slave ship hold
that was cool and dry
and did not smell

did you see me lean against a post
my legs suddenly soft
my belly cramping
a howl caught in the back of my throat

as i saw the planks that served as beds
and heard cries and moans and waves
crashing against walls
my eyes throbbing red
as shadows writhed in chains

did you hear me call out
the name i did not know
hear me whisper my thanks
to you for surviving
for keeping on
for bearing the child
who would bear the child
who would father the child
who would father me

4.

yoruba again runs strong in our line
my grandson carries it pure
from his father through my daughter
circling back to you

we are bringing you home
great grandmother
twice removed

we are bowing our heads
we are holding you close
we are learning your name

politics of identity

after Bernie Serle's installation

some days i am inside the bubbles
my image distorted by
their walls
stretched
bowed
thinned and echoed
hundreds of times
my center remaining
untouched while sheltered
by their fragile frames

some days i smash the bubbles
and they suck the bottoms of my toes
make me lose my footing
so i end up just in back of where i started

some days i am the bubbles
holding stilled wind
dressed in oiled
greens and golds shining
wet in reds and black
shimmering lightly before i
collapse

and some days
there are no bubbles
no mirrors
no reflections
no oil
no refraction
no slide
no box
no frame
no pulleys
no harness

just me
without label
without clan
without name

face covered in
sweat as i
climb
holding on
climb
getting winded
climb
being tired
climb
feeling afraid

climb
towards the sun
of myself

delphi oracle

we cross the road, trek
part way down a rocky cliff

our guide says, "drink
from this river of song
and become a poet"

i am not quite fourteen
i believe, kneel and drink
one handful of the icy water
and then another

when i next return to that place
i am just past nineteen and
the stream has been dammed

i kneel and touch the dry riverbed

smile and remind myself
to write a new poem
that very evening

love chant

you ask how are you to be sure if the poem that does not
    wear your name
was written for you who is so much more than the name
    pronounced as greg.
but things are seen and known at the center, even if their
    truth is unsaid.
you wrap around me, pull me close, seek me out each
    daybreak
we listen together to the warble and shock of morning
    birds
we call one another love names, ears open to their
    whisper.

love does not always crow, sometimes it has to whisper
short of breath and eager with a rush of words besides
    your name.
i do not know the nomenclature of the dark dawn
    singing birds
and, as you have pointed out, my poems are not
    inscribed with the crown of greg
but i am beginning to recognize those curious bird
    warbles of daybreak
patterned like our own chirping mornings with
    nothing left unsaid.

we have both said and done ugly things that cannot be
    unsaid
raged and forgotten to listen to the darkening day's
    whisper
separated by an ocean of bed we have met daybreak
me mutely, you ever watchful, vigilant as the meaning of
    greg.
and one would have thought it was a witch's cackle instead
    of the song of birds
that awoke us, if we had slept at all, with their raucous calls
    that never whisper.

i once could name more than hawk and sparrow, robin,
    owl, knew of birds
that flew these skies, remembered then so many names,
    now mostly left unsaid.
so even if unwritten these love poems hold no other name
    than greg
which you should know as you have known my breath in
    your ear as a whisper.
anyway it still is true, all said and done, what really is
    a name except a name
who we are is always what we find when the sun makes
    the day break.

even when the sky is thick with lead showing the
    grayest of daybreaks
even when the chill that nibbles our hearts is stiff
    in winter air, there are birds
and neither you or i or the woman next door knows all of
    their names.
and does it matter that we speak of their song but leave
    their title unsaid
or is what matters you and i and our trembling whispers
is what matters the truth of my love and the mirror
    reflection that is greg.

have you heard the young boys sing the chants that are
    gregorian
songs of faith, a surety of moon at night and sun at
    daybreak
sometimes inside the harshest storm you can almost hear
    their whisper
exotic and free like most unusually colored tropical
    birds.
and you know how i leave the names of deities and
    saviors unsaid
because it is only the essentials of love that need be
    named.

the night birds sing as we stroke each other beyond
    passion's whisper
creating a world where nothing is unsaid or unfelt from
    moonset to daybreak
and every poem of love i coil written or not is replete
    with the name of greg.

on issues of aliens, immigration and cosmology

1.

truth be told we are
all aliens now
traveling in outer space
on our rocky, blue sea planet

only a few of us stayed nestled
in the belly of our ancestors' birthing
on the lips of our mother's womb

all of the rest of us have traveled
to here where our heads now sleep
where our children grow and flourish
or wither and perish

but once we all were natives

long before the ones whose names
we have forgotten began their trek
we all were natives

long before the ones who stayed
stopped telling stories
of we who had left

eons ago we had no questions
about who was our kin

everyone was related

then we began to travel
turned each other
into opposites
becoming and creating
aliens

2.

we traverse this planet near the edge
of our dark milky galaxy,
rotating steadily, circling one sun
ghosted by one moon
in concert with no less than eight planets

we revolve with and without each other
and sometimes meet meteors
who whistle through star dust
creating sand storms
lake beds
mineral deposits
and fossilized amoeba

and as we move past comets
flying past us
we see stars fall
from the sky and marvel
at being in the middle
of all these galactic wonders

thus we travel
with and as aliens
in outer space on this planet
where we live

and everywhere we stay
we are surrounded
by other voyagers
like and unlike us

i know
i've always been an outsider
amidst immigrants
beside aliens
next to strangers
just like you

tempest

does the ocean understand
the land she smooths and softens

put a value on the minerals she extracts
from shells she has pounded
from bones she has chewed
from wood she has sucked
from iron she has bathed

does the ocean see her color
liquid crystal transformed
when painted by sun and dusted by silt
until she becomes gray and brown
blue and silver, sparkling green froth
as she grows and recedes
paying no attention
to the sufferance of humans
beyond offering the gift of her song
that hums in singular contentment
or howls a deep enduring sadness

does the ocean feel the shape
of each mountain she contains

how some of her lithe torso
with the gentlest of rotating currents
or through the thrusting of storms
cuts paths and rounds ridges
spoons caves and crafts nooks
where life finds sanctuary
or meets destruction

does the ocean plan her lessons

stillness without quiet
light inside darkness
how she nurtures life
and how she ends it
without pity or remorse

cosmology meditation #2

our universe
the cosmologist said
is creating itself

a quick-bread batter sky
making interstellar spaces
between raisin-sweet galaxies

our universe is not geocentric
earth at the center

nor heliocentric
sun rays spiking from
its middle

not exocentric
the center settled
a particular number of degrees
that way or this

instead we find it
omnicentric infinitely
expanding in all directions

so that wherever you are
you are at the center
of the universe

known and unknown

life creating itself
eternally stretching outward
becoming, becoming

Acknowledgments

I write alone, and been known to whine about the difficulties of group writing, always wanting my own space, spirit, rhythm and thoughts. Still this book became what it is due to the probing questions posed by Opal Palmer Adisa and Giovanni Singleton, the valuable suggestions of Nancy Peters, the thoughtful editing support of Elaine Katzenberger, the ongoing love and encouragement to write through the hardest times from my husband Gregory Harden, and the endless love and support of my children Yroko and Iwa Major Nealy. I offer my thanks and appreciation to each and all.

About the Author

A California born, San Francisco raised, granddaughter of immigrants, documented and undocumented, **devorah major** served as San Francisco's Third Poet Laureate (2002-2006). She is the author of two novels, five books of poetry, four poetry chapbooks, two young adult titles, and a host of short stories, essays, and individual poems published in anthologies and periodicals. Among her awards is a First Novelist award from the Black Caucus of the ALA and a PEN Oakland Josephine Miles Literary Award. Along with composer Guillermo Galindo, Ms. major was given a commission by the Oakland East Bay Symphony to create *Trade Routes*, a symphony with spoken word and chorus that premiered in 2005. In June 2015 she premiered her poetry play "Classic Black: Voices of 19th-Century African-Americans in San Francisco" at the San Francisco International Arts Festival. She is currently the poet-in-residence at the San Francisco Fine Arts Museums and a Senior Adjunct Professor at California College of the Arts. More info and writing can be found at www.devorahmajor.com